THIS TIME NEXT YEAR

 Kids Edition

NAME _____

YEAR _____

Co-Created by Ashton Nelson and Leading Goal Setting Expert, Romney Nelson
- The Life Graduate Publishing Group -

No part of this book may be scanned, reproduced or distributed in any printed or electronic form without the prior permission of the author or publisher.

Copyright 2020
The Life Graduate Publishing Group
and
Ashton Nelson/Romney Nelson

THIS JOURNAL INCLUDES

- Goal Setting Structure
- Fitness & Health - 12 month Goals
- Wealth Goals - 12 month Goals
- Education Goals - 12 Month Goals
- Small Steps to Achieve Your Goals
- Goal Progress Tracker
- 12 month Goal Recap
- 12 Month Goal Celebration
- What Did You Learn?

LAUNCH To Achieve Your Goals!

Goal Setting

Establishing your goals is super important as it provides us with clarity and identifies exactly what we want to achieve. Creating a goal is just the first step as we need to develop our plan on how we are going to achieve our goal. Without a plan, it is difficult to know if we are taking the right actions and we may not be headed in the direction that we need too.

DR. ACTION was created by Leading Australian Goal and Habit Development Expert Romney Nelson and is a great way to remember the steps to Goal Setting that you can use this to ensure you establish the right goals that are individual to you.

Before you create your goals, it is important that you provide 'balance' in your goals and that they are not all in one area like fitness or making money etc.

'This Time Next Year' has been created for kids to develop great goal setting habits and will provide the important balance of establishing goals across Fitness & Health, Education and Wealth Creation.

DR. ACTION

D = Dream Big. Create Big 'stretch' goals but realistic goals
R = Relevant. Create goals that 'YOU' want to achieve.
A = Action. Take action and write up your goals on paper
C = Co-ordinates. Develop your coordinates or your 'steps' for your goal
T = Time. Ensure you know 'when' you wish to achieve your goal. Be specific.
I = Implement. Commence your steps and follow your plan. Don't pause.
O = Opportunity. Look out for opportunities to progress your goals daily
N = NOW! There is no better time to start that right now.

DR. ACTION is a Trademark of 'The Life Graduate Group'

THIS TIME NEXT YEAR

GOALS

WRITE DOWN THE GOALS YOU WANT TO COMPLETE BY THIS TIME NEXT YEAR

FITNESS/HEALTH GOALS

START BY WRITING DOWN THE FIRST GOAL YOU WANT TO COMPLETE BY THIS TIME NEXT YEAR

GOAL 1

This Time Next Year I Will.....

_____

_____

_____

_____

_____

_____

_____

FITNESS/HEALTH GOALS

WHAT IS THE SECOND GOAL YOU WANT TO COMPLETE BY THIS TIME NEXT YEAR?

GOAL 2
This Time Next Year I Will.....

_____
_____
_____
_____
_____
_____
_____

FITNESS/HEALTH GOALS

WHAT IS THE THIRD GOAL YOU WANT TO COMPLETE BY THIS TIME NEXT YEAR?

GOAL 3
This Time Next Year I Will.....

_____

_____

_____

_____

_____

_____

_____

WEALTH GOALS

START BY WRITING DOWN THE FIRST GOAL YOU WANT TO COMPLETE BY THIS TIME NEXT YEAR

GOAL 1

This Time Next Year I Will.....

_____

_____

_____

_____

_____

_____

_____

WEALTH GOALS

WHAT IS THE SECOND GOAL YOU WANT TO COMPLETE BY THIS TIME NEXT YEAR?

GOAL 2

This Time Next Year I Will.....

_____

_____

_____

_____

_____

_____

_____

WEALTH GOALS

WHAT IS THE THIRD GOAL YOU WANT TO COMPLETE BY THIS TIME NEXT YEAR?

GOAL 3

This Time Next Year I Will.....

_____

_____

_____

_____

_____

_____

_____

EDUCATION GOALS

START BY WRITING DOWN THE FIRST GOAL YOU WANT TO COMPLETE BY THIS TIME NEXT YEAR

GOAL 1

This Time Next Year I Will.....

_____

_____

_____

_____

_____

_____

_____

EDUCATION GOALS

WHAT IS THE SECOND GOAL YOU WANT TO COMPLETE BY THIS TIME NEXT YEAR?

GOAL 2

This Time Next Year I Will.....

_____

_____

_____

_____

_____

_____

_____

EDUCATION GOALS

WHAT IS THE THIRD GOAL YOU WANT TO COMPLETE BY THIS TIME NEXT YEAR?

GOAL 3

This Time Next Year I Will.....

_____

_____

_____

_____

_____

_____

_____

THIS TIME NEXT YEAR

SMALL STEPS

WRITE DOWN THE LITTLE STEPS THAT YOU WILL USE TO SUCCEED IN EACH GOAL BY THIS TIME NEXT YEAR.

SMALL STEPS

in this section, you need to think about the small steps or 'mini' actions you will need to take to achieve your goal.

Establishing a goal is the first step, but without developing a plan, it is hard to know if you are on track and progressing in the right direction.

The best way is to begin at the end and then work backwards. Yes, it sounds strange but this process will help you fill in the 'missing gaps' or actions you need to take. It is like a road map but for goals.

Example:
GOAL: To save $500 over 12 months
List down your WHY? Why is your goal important to you?
Process: Think of what you will need to achieve your $500 target. Will you need to do some small jobs for family, friends or neighbors to get some money? Are you old enough to get a casual job? Do you need to change your attitude towards how you use your money and are you spending all of it as soon as you get it? Eg Money from birthdays or a casual job?

Step 1 - I calculate that I need to save $10.00 per week (or close to it)
Step 2 - I need to think of a way I can get some extra pocket money. eg. Washing house windows, cars or gain a casual job. (create some actions to make this happen.
Step 3 - I get a large tin and place 'My $500 Savings Goal'
Step 4 - I get a small notepad and each time I contribute to the tin, I write down how much I place in it.
Step 5 - I make a commitment to place $10.00 p/week in my tin and never to open the tin until the end of the year.
Step 6 - If I feel comfortable doing so, I share my goal with someone I trust and therefore they can help encourage me to keep saving towards my goal.

FITNESS/HEALTH SMALL STEPS

WRITE DOWN THE LITTLE STEPS THAT YOU WILL USE TO SUCCEED IN EACH GOAL BY THIS TIME NEXT YEAR.

GOAL 1
This Time Next Year I Will.....

_____

_____

_____

_____

_____

_____

_____

Tip: Use 5 - 10 dot points for each goal of the little steps or actions you need to take to achieve your goal. The little steps will lead you to the path of achieving your goal.

FITNESS/HEALTH SMALL STEPS

Note down your steps and plan

GOAL 2
This Time Next Year I Will.....

_____
_____
_____
_____
_____
_____
_____
_____

FITNESS/HEALTH SMALL STEPS

Note down your steps and plan

GOAL 3
This Time Next Year I Will.....

_____
_____
_____
_____
_____
_____
_____
_____

WEALTH SMALL STEPS

WRITE DOWN THE LITTLE STEPS THAT YOU WILL USE TO SUCCEED IN EACH GOAL BY THIS TIME NEXT YEAR.

This Time Next Year I Will.....

_____

_____

_____

_____

_____

_____

_____

WEALTH SMALL STEPS

Note down your steps and plan

GOAL 2
This Time Next Year I Will.....

_____
_____
_____
_____
_____
_____
_____
_____

WEALTH SMALL STEPS

Note down your steps and plan

GOAL 3
This Time Next Year I Will.....

_____

_____

_____

_____

_____

_____

_____

EDUCATION SMALL STEPS

WRITE DOWN THE LITTLE STEPS THAT YOU WILL USE TO SUCCEED IN EACH GOAL BY THIS TIME NEXT YEAR.

GOAL 1
This Time Next Year I Will.....

___
___
___
___
___
___
___
___

EDUCATION SMALL STEPS

Note down your steps and plan

GOAL 2
This Time Next Year I Will.....

_____
_____
_____
_____
_____
_____
_____
_____

EDUCATION SMALL STEPS

Note down your steps and plan

GOAL 3
This Time Next Year I Will.....

_____
_____
_____
_____
_____
_____
_____
_____

THIS TIME NEXT YEAR

PROGRESS

Note your progress below. Are you on track to achieve your goal? Are there things you should start doing, stop doing or continue to do?

FITNESS/HEALTH PROGRESS

Note your progress below. Are you on track to achieve your goal? Are there things you should start doing, stop doing or continue to do?

MONTH 1

this month i have.....

_____

_____

_____

_____

_____

_____

_____

WEALTH PROGRESS

NOTE YOUR PROGRESS BELOW. ARE YOU ON TRACK TO ACHIEVE YOUR GOAL? ARE THERE THINGS YOU SHOULD START DOING, STOP DOING OR CONTINUE TO DO?

MONTH 1
this month i have.....

_____

_____

_____

_____

_____

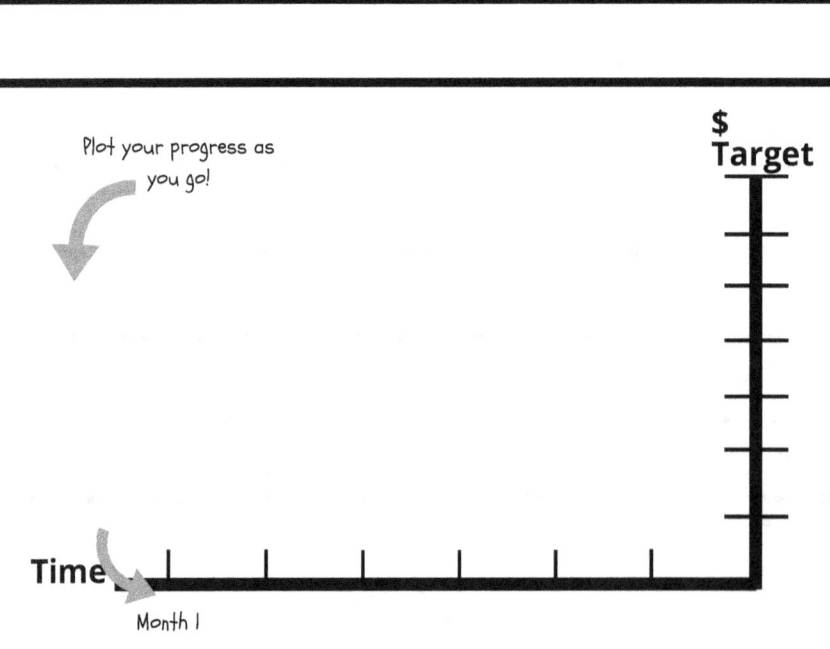

EDUCATION PROGRESS

Note your progress below. Are you on track to achieve your goal? Are there things you should start doing, stop doing or continue to do?

MONTH 1
this month i have.....

_____
_____
_____
_____
_____
_____
_____
_____

FITNESS/HEALTH PROGRESS

Note your progress below. Are you on track to achieve your goal? Are there things you should start doing, stop doing or continue to do?

MONTH 2
this month i have.....

_____
_____
_____
_____
_____
_____
_____

WEALTH PROGRESS

Note your progress below. Are you on track to achieve your goal? Are there things you should start doing, stop doing or continue to do?

MONTH 2
this month i have.....

_____
_____
_____
_____

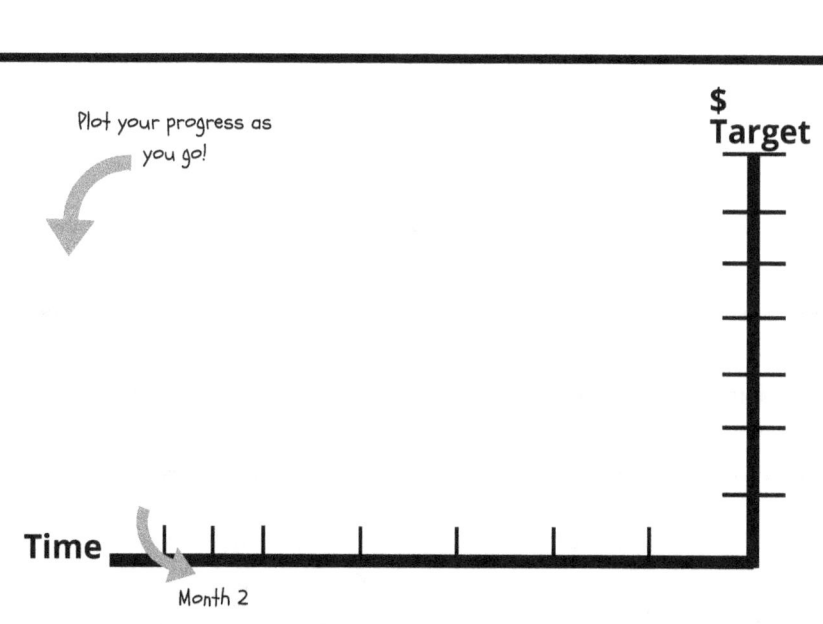

EDUCATION PROGRESS

Note your progress below. Are you on track to achieve your goal? Are there things you should start doing, stop doing or continue to do?

MONTH 2
this month i have.....

_____

_____

_____

_____

_____

_____

_____

_____

FITNESS/HEALTH PROGRESS

Note your progress below. Are you on track to achieve your goal? Are there things you should start doing, stop doing or continue to do?

MONTH 3
this month i have.....

_____
_____
_____
_____
_____
_____
_____
_____

WEALTH PROGRESS

Note your progress below. Are you on track to achieve your goal? Are there things you should start doing, stop doing or continue to do?

MONTH 3
this month i have.....

_____
_____
_____
_____

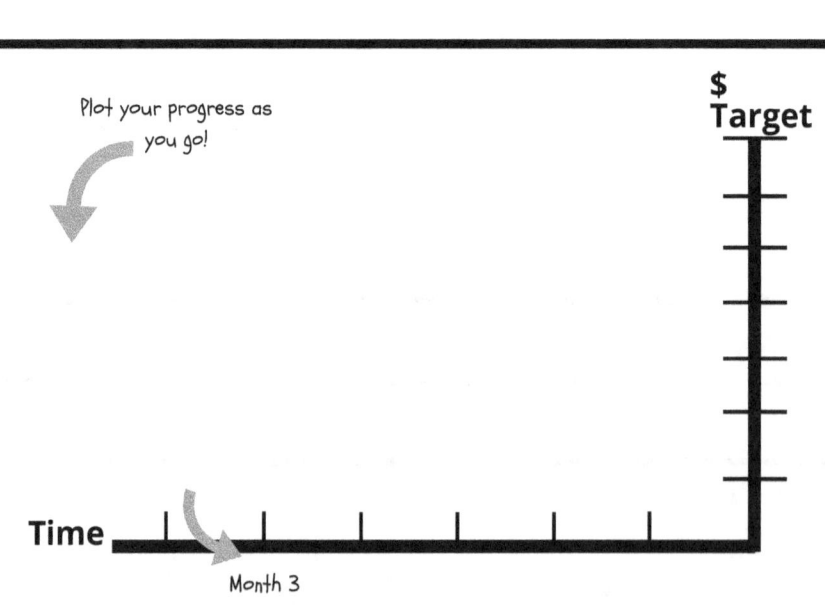

EDUCATION PROGRESS

Note your progress below. Are you on track to achieve your goal? Are there things you should start doing, stop doing or continue to do?

this month i have.....

_____
_____
_____
_____
_____
_____
_____

FITNESS/HEALTH PROGRESS

Note your progress below. Are you on track to achieve your goal? Are there things you should start doing, stop doing or continue to do?

MONTH 4
this month i have.....

_____

_____

_____

_____

_____

_____

_____

_____

WEALTH PROGRESS

Note your progress below. Are you on track to achieve your goal? Are there things you should start doing, stop doing or continue to do?

this month i have.....

_____

_____

_____

_____

_____

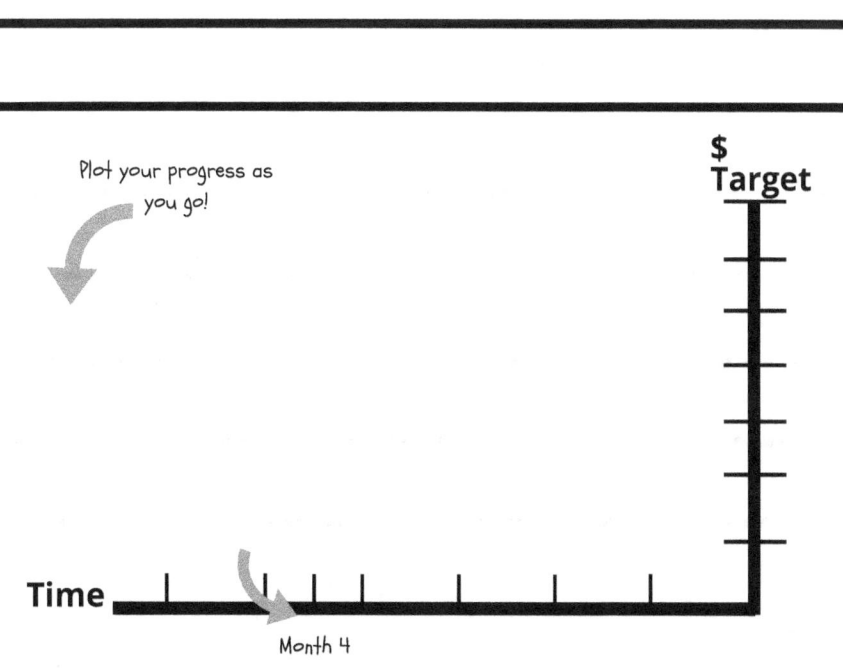

EDUCATION PROGRESS

Note your progress below. Are you on track to achieve your goal? Are there things you should start doing, stop doing or continue to do?

MONTH 4

this month i have.....

_____
_____
_____
_____
_____
_____
_____

FITNESS/HEALTH PROGRESS

Note your progress below. Are you on track to achieve your goal? Are there things you should start doing, stop doing or continue to do?

MONTH 5
this month i have.....

WEALTH PROGRESS

NOTE YOUR PROGRESS BELOW. ARE YOU ON TRACK TO ACHIEVE YOUR GOAL? ARE THERE THINGS YOU SHOULD START DOING, STOP DOING OR CONTINUE TO DO?

MONTH 5
this month i have.....

_____

_____

_____

_____

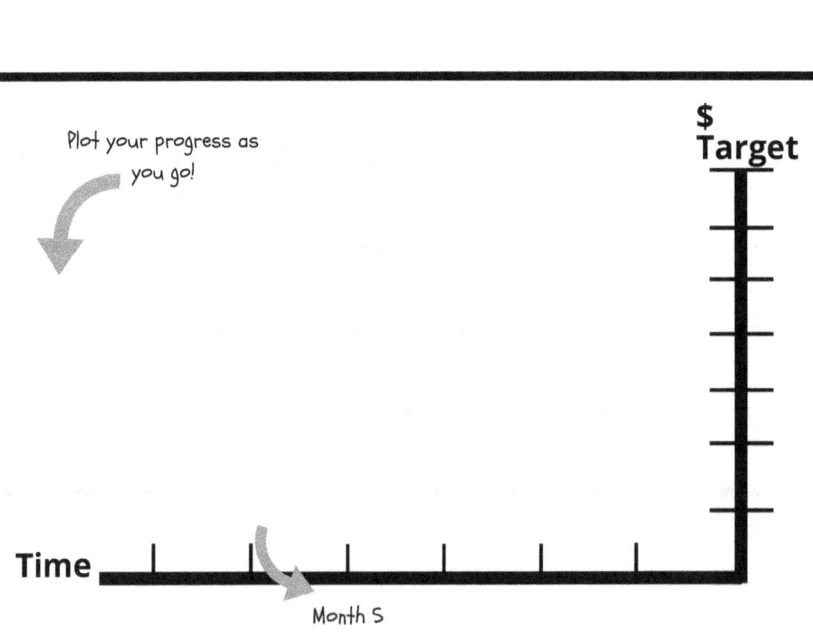

EDUCATION PROGRESS

Note your progress below. Are you on track to achieve your goal? Are there things you should start doing, stop doing or continue to do?

MONTH 5
this month i have.....

_____
_____
_____
_____
_____
_____
_____

FITNESS/HEALTH PROGRESS

Note your progress below. Are you on track to achieve your goal? Are there things you should start doing, stop doing or continue to do?

MONTH 6

this month i have.....

_____

_____

_____

_____

_____

_____

_____

WEALTH PROGRESS

NOTE YOUR PROGRESS BELOW. ARE YOU ON TRACK TO ACHIEVE YOUR GOAL? ARE THERE THINGS YOU SHOULD START DOING, STOP DOING OR CONTINUE TO DO?

MONTH 6
this month i have.....

_____
_____
_____
_____

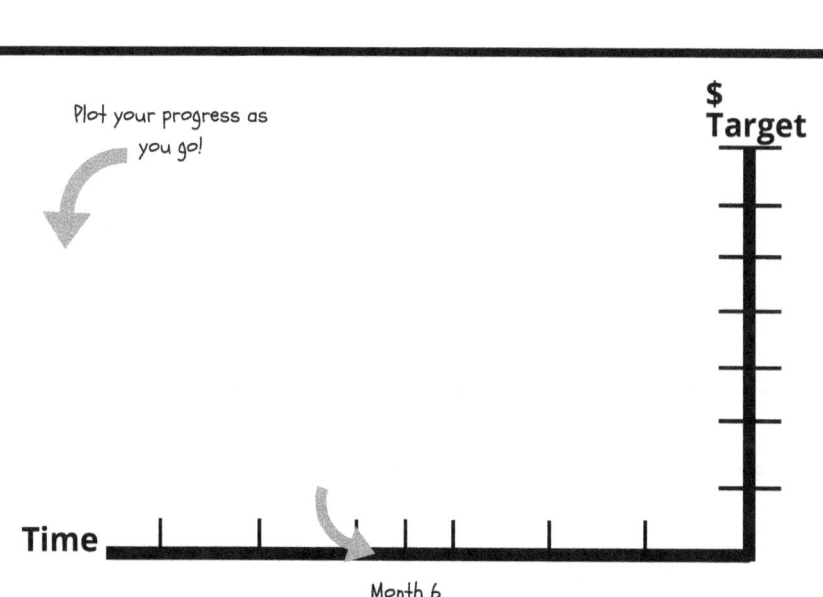

EDUCATION PROGRESS

Note your progress below. Are you on track to achieve your goal? Are there things you should start doing, stop doing or continue to do?

MONTH 6
this month i have.....

_____
_____
_____
_____
_____
_____
_____
_____

FITNESS/HEALTH PROGRESS

Note your progress below. Are you on track to achieve your goal? Are there things you should start doing, stop doing or continue to do?

this month i have.....

_____

_____

_____

_____

_____

_____

_____

WEALTH PROGRESS

Note your progress below. Are you on track to achieve your goal? Are there things you should start doing, stop doing or continue to do?

MONTH 7
this month i have.....

_____
_____
_____
_____

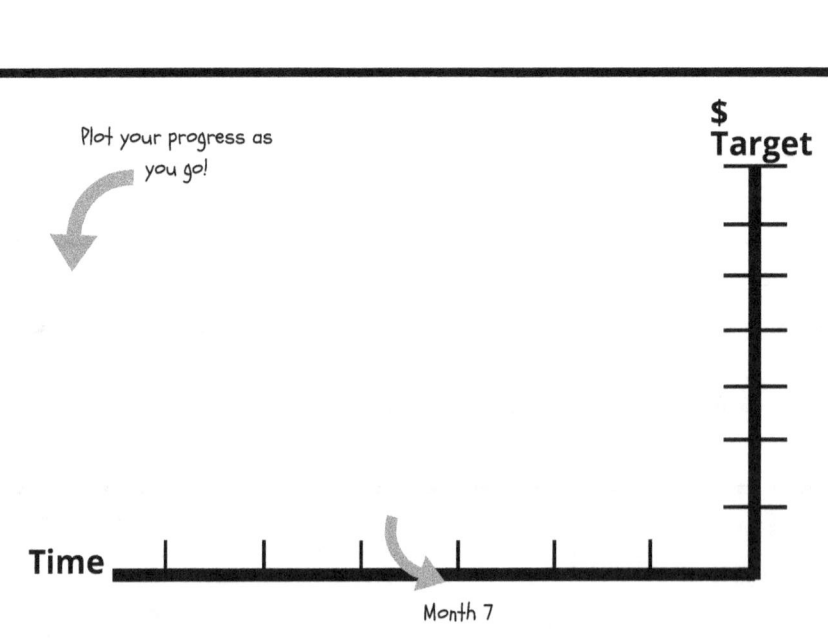

Plot your progress as you go!

$ Target

Time

Month 7

EDUCATION PROGRESS

Note your progress below. Are you on track to achieve your goal? Are there things you should start doing, stop doing or continue to do?

MONTH 7
this month i have.....

_____
_____
_____
_____
_____
_____
_____

FITNESS/HEALTH PROGRESS

Note your progress below. Are you on track to achieve your goal? Are there things you should start doing, stop doing or continue to do?

MONTH 8
this month i have.....

_____
_____
_____
_____
_____
_____
_____
_____

WEALTH PROGRESS

Note your progress below. Are you on track to achieve your goal? Are there things you should start doing, stop doing or continue to do?

MONTH 8

this month i have.....

_____
_____
_____
_____
_____

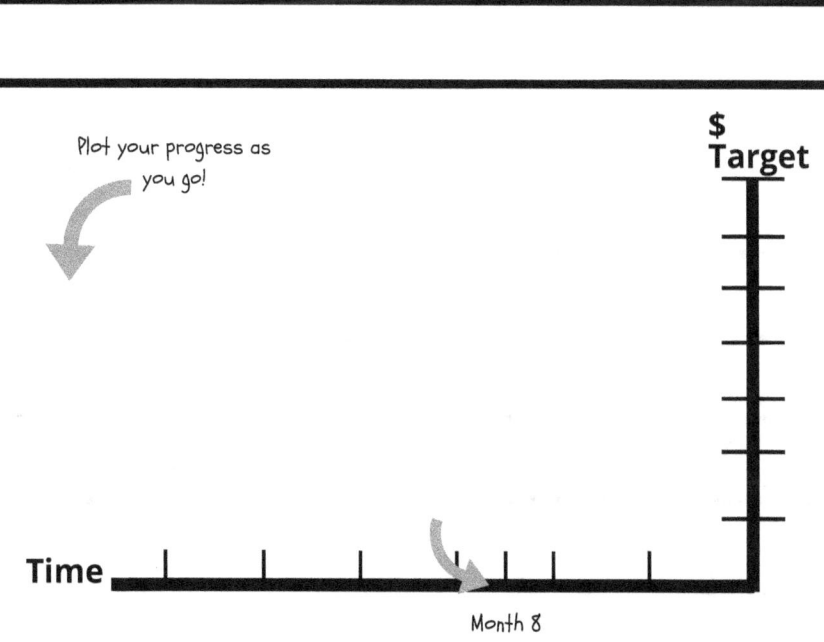

EDUCATION PROGRESS

Note your progress below. Are you on track to achieve your goal? Are there things you should start doing, stop doing or continue to do?

MONTH 8
this month i have.....

_____

_____

_____

_____

_____

_____

_____

FITNESS/HEALTH PROGRESS

Note your progress below. Are you on track to achieve your goal? Are there things you should start doing, stop doing or continue to do?

MONTH 9
this month i have.....

_____

_____

_____

_____

_____

_____

_____

_____

WEALTH PROGRESS

NOTE YOUR PROGRESS BELOW. ARE YOU ON TRACK TO ACHIEVE YOUR GOAL? ARE THERE THINGS YOU SHOULD START DOING, STOP DOING OR CONTINUE TO DO?

MONTH 9

this month i have.....

_____

_____

_____

_____

_____

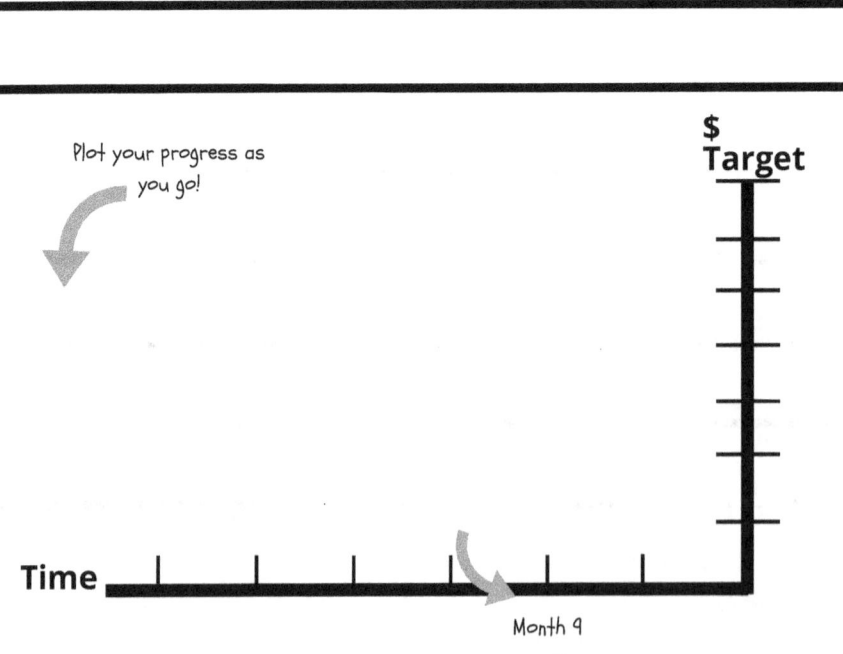

EDUCATION PROGRESS

Note your progress below. Are you on track to achieve your goal? Are there things you should start doing, stop doing or continue to do?

MONTH 9
this month i have.....

FITNESS/HEALTH PROGRESS

Note your progress below. Are you on track to achieve your goal? Are there things you should start doing, stop doing or continue to do?

MONTH 10
this month i have.....

_____
_____
_____
_____
_____
_____
_____

WEALTH PROGRESS

Note your progress below. Are you on track to achieve your goal? Are there things you should start doing, stop doing or continue to do?

MONTH 10
this month i have.....

_____
_____
_____
_____
_____

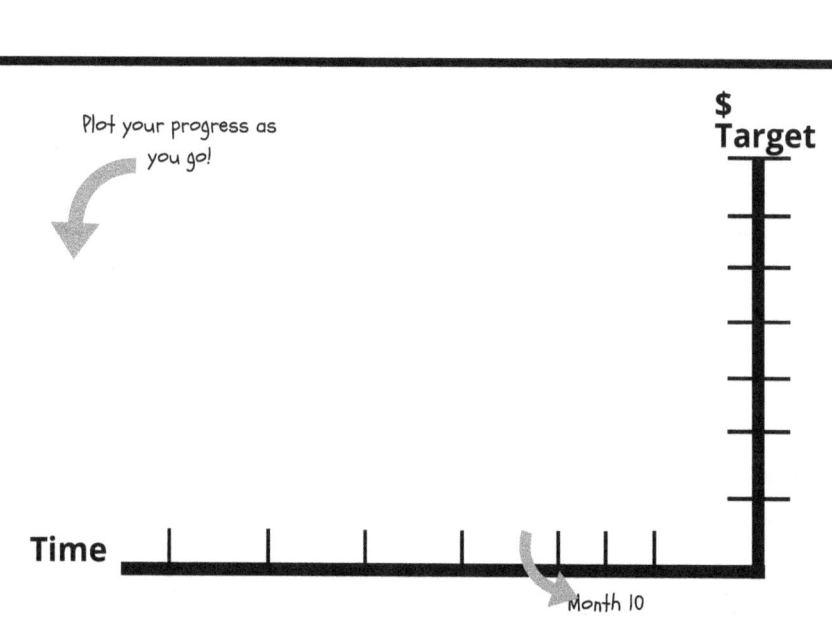

EDUCATION PROGRESS

Note your progress below. Are you on track to achieve your goal? Are there things you should start doing, stop doing or continue to do?

MONTH 10
this month i have.....

_____
_____
_____
_____
_____
_____
_____
_____

FITNESS/HEALTH PROGRESS

Note your progress below. Are you on track to achieve your goal? Are there things you should start doing, stop doing or continue to do?

this month i have.....

_____
_____
_____
_____
_____
_____
_____

WEALTH PROGRESS

Note your progress below. Are you on track to achieve your goal? Are there things you should start doing, stop doing or continue to do?

MONTH 11
this month i have.....

_____
_____
_____
_____
_____

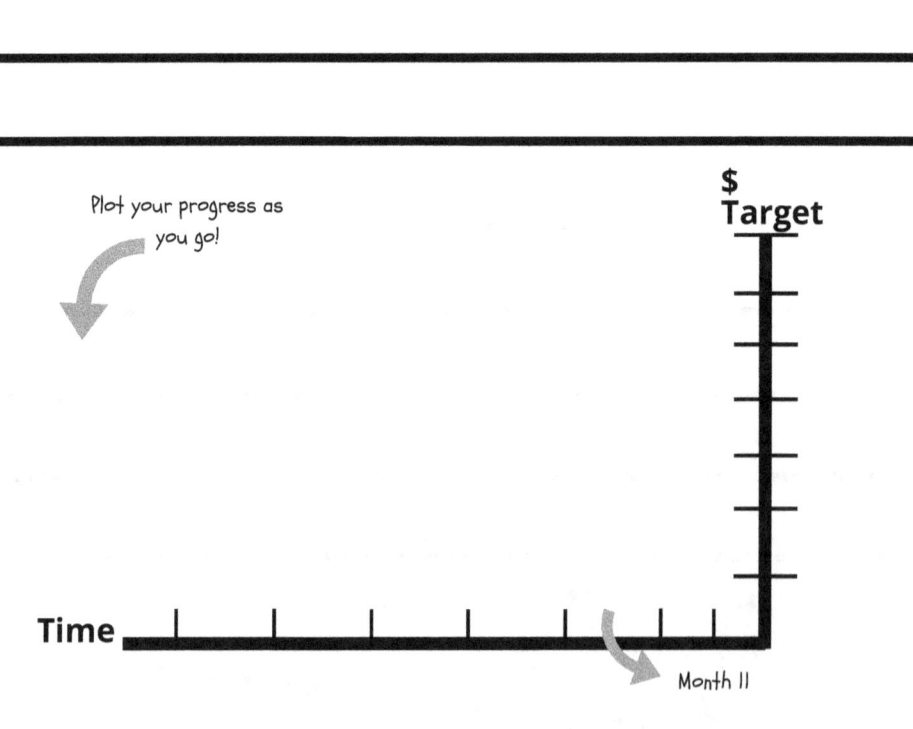

Plot your progress as you go!

$ Target

Time

Month 11

EDUCATION PROGRESS

Note your progress below. Are you on track to achieve your goal? Are there things you should start doing, stop doing or continue to do?

MONTH 11

this month i have.....

_____
_____
_____
_____
_____
_____
_____
_____
_____

THIS TIME NEXT YEAR

12 MONTH RECAP

YOU HAVE COMPLETED YOUR 12 MONTHS OF GOALS. HOW FAR HAVE YOU COME?

FITNESS/HEALTH RECAP

WRITE DOWN HOW FAR YOU HAVE PROGRESSED THROUGH EVERY MONTH. ARE YOU HAPPY WITH YOUR PROGRESS?

MONTH 12

this year i have.....

_____

_____

_____

_____

_____

_____

_____

_____

WEALTH RECAP

WRITE DOWN HOW FAR YOU HAVE PROGRESSED THROUGH EVERY MONTH. ARE YOU HAPPY WITH YOUR PROGRESS?

MONTH 12
this year i have.....

_____
_____
_____
_____

DID YOU HIT YOUR TARGET?

$ Target

Time

EDUCATION RECAP

WRITE DOWN HOW FAR YOU HAVE PROGRESSED THROUGH EVERY MONTH. ARE YOU HAPPY WITH YOUR PROGRESS?

MONTH 12

this year i have.....

_____
_____
_____
_____
_____
_____
_____
_____

THIS TIME NEXT YEAR

CELEBRATION

YOU HAVE COMPLETED YOUR 12 MONTH TRACKER.

CONGRATULATIONS!

CELEBRATION!

YOU HAVE COMPLETED YOUR 12 MONTHS OF GOALS! HOW FAR HAVE YOU COME? HOW WILL YOU CELEBRATE!

I have come so far and I will celebrate by.....

_____
_____
_____
_____
_____
_____
_____
_____
_____
_____
_____
_____

What did you learn?

Do you have anything else you would like to write down about your year? Some sugestions:
- What challenges did you encounter?
- What would you have done differently?
- What important lessons did you learn during the process?

___

Order your next copy of

AVAILABLE ON ALL
MAJOR ONLINE BOOKSTORES
or via
www.thelifegraduate.com

www.ingramcontent.com/pod-product-compliance
Lightning Source LLC
LaVergne TN
LVHW060143080526
838202LV00049B/4065